THE WORLD'S TOP TEN

LAKES

Neil Morris

Illustrated by Vanessa Card

Chrysalis Children's Books

Words in **bold** are explained in the glossary
on pages 30–31.

This edition published in 2003 by
Chrysalis Children's Books
The Chrysalis Building, Bramley Road,
London W10 6SP

ISBN 1 84138 484 4

British Library Cataloguing in Publication Data for this book
is available from the British Library.

Editor: Maria O'Neill
Designer: Dawn Apperley
Picture Researcher: Diana Morris
Consultant: Elizabeth M Lewis

Printed in China By Imago

Picture acknowledgements:
J Allan Cash: 16, 17, 24, 26, 27, 29t.
James Davis Photography: 5b, 28b, 29b.
Eye Ubiquitous: 5t & 11 © L Fordyce, 15 © K Mullineaux.
First Light: 10 © Grant Black, 14 © Alan Marsh.
Lyn Hancock: 22, 23.
Robert Harding Picture Library: 18.
Hutchison Picture Library: 8 © A Grachtchenkov, 21 ©
Crispin Hughes. Link: 20 © Ron Gilrig. Novosti: 9.
Panos: 19 © Marcus Rose.
Still Pictures: 13 © T de Sallis, 25 © Hjalte Tiu.
Trip: 12 © Johnson Hicks, 28t © Eric Smith.

Contents

What is a lake?

A lake is a body of water that is surrounded by land. Lakes form in hollows in the Earth's surface, called **basins**. Lake water comes from rainfall and melting snow. Much of the water flows into the basin as rivers and streams. Most lakes are full of **fresh water**, but the biggest lake in the world is salty.

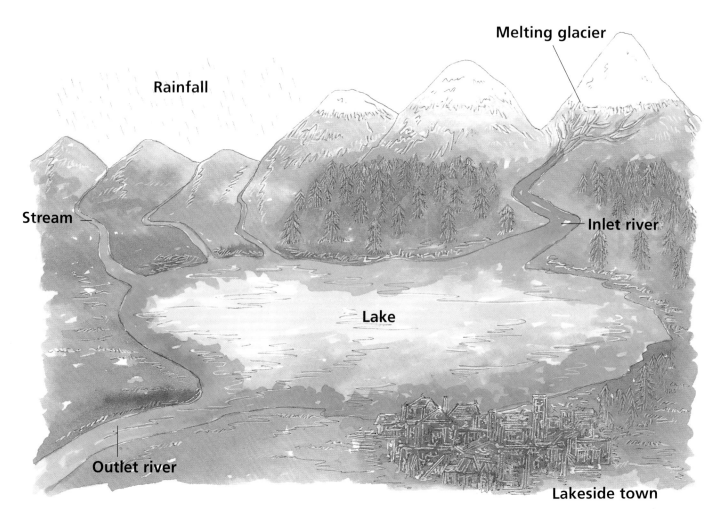

Rainfall

Melting glacier

Stream

Inlet river

Lake

Outlet river

Lakeside town

How lakes form

Many lakes are in areas that were once covered by rivers of ice, called **glaciers**. The glaciers made hollows in the ground as they moved. When the ice melted, these basins filled with water.

Other lake basins formed when the Earth's **crust** moved. **Volcanoes**, **earthquakes** and moving cracks in the crust made hollows that filled with water from rivers or underground **springs**.

Crater Lake, in the US state of Oregon, formed when rain and melting snow filled the crater of a volcano thousands of years ago. The island in the lake is the tip of another smaller volcano.

Lake dwellers

We have learned a lot by digging up remains of **settlements** near lakes and finding out how ancient people lived. Thousands of years ago, people in Europe sometimes built houses over the water at the edge of lakes.

The houses were on wooden platforms that stood on posts driven into the **lake bed**. These early people lived by lakes because water and **transport** were in good supply. In some parts of the world, people still live in stilt houses on lakes.

The biggest lakes

In this book we take a look at the ten biggest lakes in the world. We see how different they are from each other and get to know the people and animals who have made lakes and lakeshores their homes.

The ancient town of Sirmione lies on the shores of Lake Garda, in northern Italy. Ancient **ruins** of Roman houses have been found here, dating back more than 2000 years.

The biggest lakes

This map shows where the ten biggest lakes are in the world. These are the lakes with the largest surface area, measured in square kilometres. The biggest of all is the Caspian Sea and it is a salt-water lake. It is more than four times bigger than Lake Superior, the next lake on the list. When you stand on the shores of the Caspian Sea, you cannot see the land on the other side so it looks more like the sea than a lake. Number nine in our list, Lake Baikal, is the world's deepest lake and holds the most fresh water.

The world's top ten lakes

1 Caspian Sea	371 800	sq km
2 Lake Superior	82 350	sq km
3 Lake Victoria	69 500	sq km
4 Lake Huron	59 600	sq km
5 Lake Michigan	58 000	sq km
6 Aral Sea	37 000	sq km
7 Lake Tanganyika	32 900	sq km
8 Great Bear Lake	31 800	sq km
9 Lake Baikal	30 500	sq km
10 Lake Malawi	29 600	sq km

Great Bear Lake

NORTH AMERICA

Lake Superior

Lake Michigan

Lake Huron

ATLANTIC OCEAN

SOUTH AMERICA

PACIFIC OCEAN

ARCTIC
OCEAN

EUROPE

PACIFIC
OCEAN

Lake Baikal

Aral Sea

ASIA

Caspian Sea

AFRICA

Lake Victoria

INDIAN
OCEAN

Lake Tanganyika

Lake Malawi

AUSTRALIA

ATLANTIC
OCEAN

ANTARCTICA

Caspian Sea

The Caspian Sea is the largest lake in the world. Scientists believe that it is probably the world's oldest lake too. Many rivers flow into this huge **salt-water** lake, including Europe's longest river, the Volga. But not a single river flows out of it.

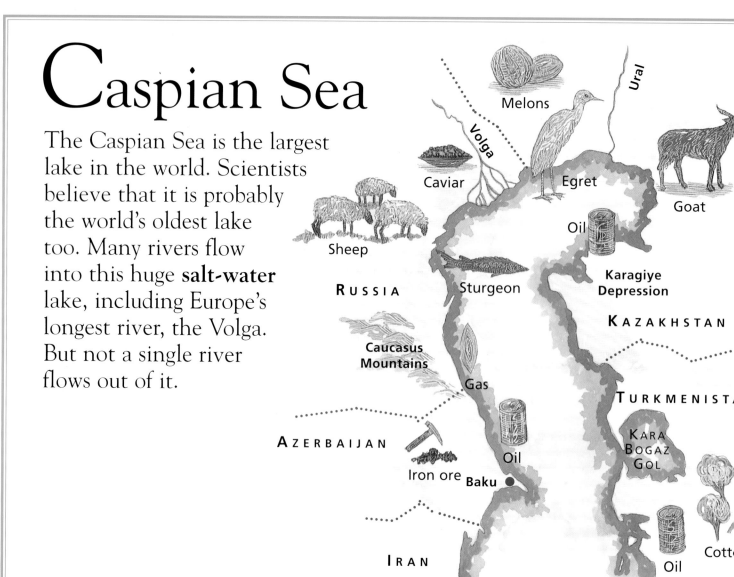

Melons

Ural

Volga

Caviar

Egret

Goat

Oil

Karagiye Depression

Sheep

RUSSIA

Sturgeon

KAZAKHSTAN

Caucasus Mountains

Gas

TURKMENISTAN

AZERBAIJAN

KARA BOGAZ GOL

Oil

Iron ore   Baku ●

Cott

IRAN

Oil

Lizard

Elburz Mountains

Russian fishermen set their nets in the River Volga, trying to catch fish swimming to the Caspian Sea. The fishermen's most valuable catch is the sturgeon.

Salt water

The River Volga flows for over 3500 kilometres before it empties into the Caspian Sea. Near the Volga **delta**, the lake's water is almost free of salt. Most of the lake's water is less salty than normal seawater. In the shallow **gulf** called Kara Bogaz Gol, the water is ten times as salty as seawater. There the lake bed is covered by a layer of salt two metres thick.

Between Europe and Asia

The Ural Mountains form the border between the **continents** of Europe and Asia. At the southern end of the mountains, the Ural River flows to the Caspian Sea. The lake's eastern and southern shores belong to Kazakhstan, Turkmenistan and Iran.

The western and northern shores belong to Azerbaijan, Russia and Kazakhstan. The land surrounding the lake ranges from the Caucasus and Elburz Mountains to the Karagiye Depression. The surface of the lake lies 28 metres below **sea level**.

FACTS

AREA	371 800 sq km
GREATEST LENGTH	1225 km
GREATEST DEPTH	1025 m
ALTITUDE	-28 m
LOCATION	Azerbaijan, Iran, Russia, Kazakhstan, Turkmenistan

The wind has whipped up the Caspian Sea so that surf breaks on the shores of Turkmenistan. This makes the world's largest lake look like an ocean.

Oil production

Once the Caspian was famous for caviar, the **roe** of the sturgeon. But fishing and industrial **pollution** have reduced the number of fish in the lake. Now the lake's most important **resources** are oil and natural gas. Companies drill for oil on the shore and beneath the waters of the lake. The Caspian countries want to increase their oil production, but many people are worried that the lake could become more polluted.

Lake Superior

Lake Superior is the biggest and deepest of the five Great Lakes of North America, and is the largest freshwater lake in the world. The lake lies on the border between the United States and Canada, and the **national boundary** runs right across it.

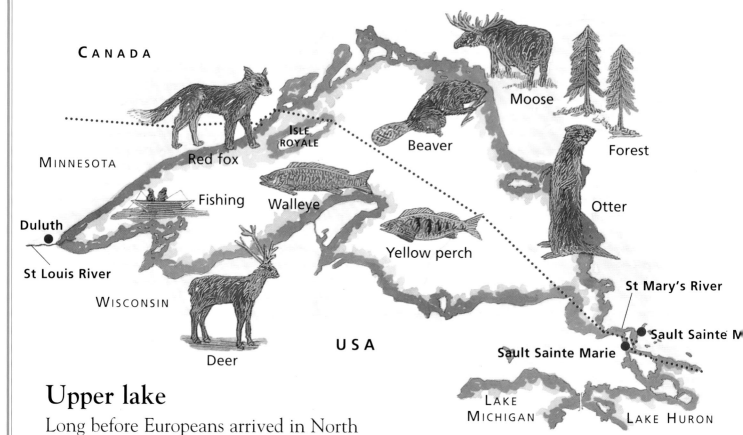

CANADA

MINNESOTA

Red fox

ISLE ROYALE

Duluth

St Louis River

WISCONSIN

Fishing

Walleye

Beaver

Moose

Forest

Otter

Yellow perch

Deer

USA

St Mary's River

Sault Sainte M

Sault Sainte Marie

LAKE MICHIGAN

LAKE HURON

Upper lake

Long before Europeans arrived in North America, Ojibwa and Menomini Indian tribes lived around the lake's shores. The Ojibwa used birch bark to build **wigwams** and canoes and lived on otter, beaver and fish from the lake. In 1622, the French explorer Étienne Brûlé reached the lake, and he was followed by fur traders. They called the lake Lac Supérieur, which means Upper Lake.

Icy waves break on the Canadian shore of Lake Superior. The lake does not completely freeze over in winter, but **harbours** are usually iced up for at least three months.

A ship enters one of the Soo Canal locks, where the water level is lowered and raised to let ships pass through.

FACTS

AREA	82 350 sq km
GREATEST LENGTH	560 km
GREATEST DEPTH	406 m
ALTITUDE	183 m
LOCATION	Canada, USA

Flowing in and out

About 200 rivers flow into Lake Superior. The largest is the St Louis River, at the western end of the lake. At the eastern end, the lake flows into the St Mary's River, which links it to Lake Huron, the fourth biggest lake in the world. Lake Superior lies 183 metres above sea level, which is seven metres higher than Lake Huron. To avoid **rapids** on St Mary's River, ships pass through the five **locks** of the Soo Canals at the twin towns of Sault Sainte Marie.

Rocky shores and islands

Lake Superior is surrounded by a rocky coastline and beautiful forests. At Pictured Rocks National Lakeshore, in Michigan, multicoloured sandstone cliffs rise up to 60 metres for a stretch of 24 kilometres. Wind and rain have carved the cliffs into strange shapes. The lake's largest island, Isle Royale, is a US **national park**. Beavers, snowshoe hares and red foxes live on the island.

11

Lake Victoria

Victoria is the largest lake in Africa and the third largest lake in the world. Lake Victoria has the highest **altitude** of the world's top ten lakes. It lies on the **Equator** and is divided mainly between the countries of Uganda and Tanzania. A small part of its waters and shoreline belong to Kenya.

Victoria Nile

UGANDA

Dam

Jinja

EQUATOR

Entebbe

Kisu

Shipping

Crocodile

Nile perch

KENYA

Flamingo

Cichlids

Kagera

Lily trotter

TANZANIA

Mwanza

Freshwater jellyfish

Source of the Nile

In 1858, an English explorer called John Hanning Speke went in search of the **source** of the River Nile, the longest river in the world. He came across a huge lake, which he named Lake Victoria, in honour of Queen Victoria. We now know that the true source of the Nile is a branch of the Kagera, one of the many rivers that flow into Lake Victoria. The Nile is the only river that flows out of the lake.

Lake Victoria is the shallowest of the large freshwater lakes and contains many small islands. These are the Sese Islands, off the Ugandan coast.

The Owen Falls **Dam** was built across the Victoria Nile River, near Jinja. When it opened in 1954, the dam raised the level of Lake Victoria by almost a metre. The dam is used to make electricity.

On a high plateau

The lake's surface is more than 1000 metres above sea level. The lake's waters fill a shallow basin on a high **plateau**, which formed about 750 000 years ago. This area of high land lies between two deep valleys. The valleys belong to a long series of deep cracks in the Earth's surface known as the **Great Rift Valley**.

FACTS

AREA	69 500 sq km
GREATEST LENGTH	360 km
GREATEST DEPTH	82 m
ALTITUDE	1135 m
LOCATION	Kenya, Tanzania, Uganda

Major ports

Millions of people live near the shores of Lake Victoria. Shipping services link the main ports of three countries: Mwanza in Tanzania, Entebbe in Uganda and Kisumu in Kenya. The lake is a valuable source of fish and contains 170 kinds of **tropical** fish called cichlids. Many small fish have been killed off by the Nile perch, which was introduced into the lake in 1964.

13

Lake Huron

Lake Huron is the second largest of the Great Lakes of North America. The border between the United States and Canada runs across the lake. Water flows into the lake from Lake Superior, down the St Mary's River, from Lake Michigan, through the **Straits** of Mackinac, and from other small rivers.

The Huron people

Lake Huron was the first of the Great Lakes to be discovered by Europeans. A French explorer called Samuel de Champlain reached the lake in 1615 and found Huron Indians living on its shores. French fur **traders** followed Champlain to the lake and named it after the native people.

LAKE SUPERIOR

Deer

CANADA

St Mary's River

Black bear

LAKE MICHIGAN

Straits of Mackinac

Lake trout

MANITOULIN

Chipmu

USA

Beaver

GEORGIAN BAY

Belted kingfisher

MICHIGAN

Shipping

Pine forest

Racoon

Silver maple

Port Huron

Sarnia

St Clair River

Forests grow along the shore of Lake Huron in Ontario, Canada. Before Europeans arrived, the Huron people lived in villages in lakeside forests of blue beech, white pine and silver maple.

Facts

AREA	59 600 sq km
GREATEST LENGTH	330 km
GREATEST DEPTH	229m
ALTITUDE	176m
LOCATION	Canada, USA

Saint Lawrence Seaway

Lake Huron and the other Great Lakes form part of a waterway that allows ships to sail over 3700 kilometres from the Atlantic Ocean to the port of Duluth on Lake Superior. This waterway is called the St Lawrence Seaway. Ice on the lakes usually stops shipping from January to March each year.

Large islands

Like all the Great Lakes and most lakes around the world, Huron is dotted with islands. Most lie in the northern part of the lake, especially in Georgian Bay. The two biggest islands are Mackinac, in the American section of the lake, and Manitoulin, which belongs to Canada. Manitoulin is the largest freshwater island in the world. It is 129 kilometres long and is covered in forest. The Manitoulin islanders make a living from tourism as well as timber.

This group of Georgian Bay islands form a national park. The forests and wildlife in national parks are protected. Some small human settlements can be seen from the air.

15

Lake Michigan

Lake Michigan is the third largest of the Great Lakes of North America. It lies entirely within the United States and is bordered by four different states: Michigan to the north and east, Wisconsin to the west, and Illinois and Indiana to the south.

The shores of Lake Michigan have changed since the Menomini people lived there. This marina outside Chicago is a place where tourists and local people enjoy boating for leisure.

LAKE SUPERIOR

Loon

Straits of Mackinac

Beaver

Walleye

MANITOU ISLANDS

Forest

American football

Green Bay

Snapping turtle

Sleeping Bear Dunes

WISCONSIN

Polish dancer

Lake herring

Frog

Milwaukee

MICHIGAN

Basketball

Skyscrapers

Duck

ILLINOIS

INDIANA

Chicago

Chicago River

European explorers

Menomini and other Indian tribes lived near the shores of the lake long before European explorers and fur-trappers arrived. A Frenchman called Jean Nicolet was the first European to reach the area, in 1634. He set out to explore the lake, thinking that he would end up in China. When his canoe reached land, he went ashore wearing a Chinese robe. In fact he had landed on the Wisconsin side of Lake Michigan, the home of native Americans.

A lakeside view of Chicago shows some of the tallest buildings in the world. The modern **skyscraper** was invented in this great city.

City ports

All four states around the lake have large, busy ports. Milwaukee, the chief port and industrial centre of Wisconsin, has a population of 1.6 million. The biggest lakeside port of all is Chicago, in Illinois, which is the third largest city in the United States and has a population of 8 million. The city is divided by the Chicago River, which flows out of the lake. The Chicago and Illinois rivers, together with the Chicago Sanitary and Ship Canal, link Lake Michigan to the Mississippi River.

FACTS

AREA	58 000 sq km
GREATEST LENGTH	494 km
GREATEST DEPTH	281 m
ALTITUDE	176m
LOCATION	USA

Sleeping Bear Dunes

On the other side of the lake, there is a towering mass of sand dunes. These dunes cover 50 kilometres of shoreline, and some are 135 metres high. This part of Michigan is now protected. It is called Sleeping Bear Dunes National Lakeshore. The name comes from a huge hill of sand that is shaped like a bear at rest.

Aral Sea

The Aral Sea lies about 400 kilometres east of the Caspian Sea, between Uzbekistan and Kazakhstan. It has slipped from fourth to sixth in the list of the world's largest lakes because it is shrinking. Water from the rivers that feed the lake has been diverted into man-made canals. Every year the lake's water level drops and its shoreline moves back.

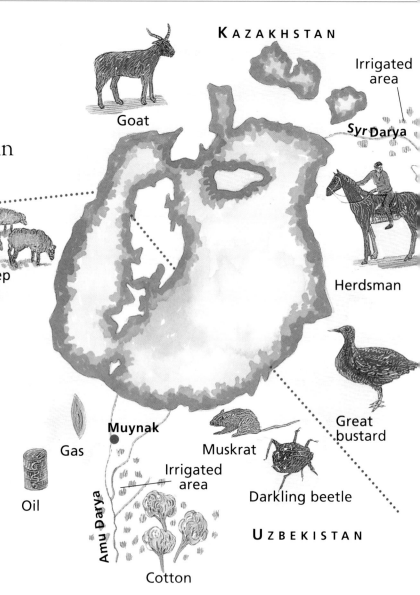

KAZAKHSTAN

Goat

Irrigated area

Syr Darya

Sheep

Herdsman

Gas

Oil

Muynak

Amu Darya

Irrigated area

Muskrat

Darkling beetle

Great bustard

Cotton

UZBEKISTAN

The River Amu Darya flows through Uzbekistan towards the Aral Sea. Today, its waters scarcely reach the shrinking lake.

Sea of islands

The lake's name means 'sea of islands'. Just 30 years ago, the Aral contained over 1100 small islands. Many of these have now joined together as the water level drops. The lake's water comes from two rivers, the Amu Darya and the Syr Darya. In 1980 the Karakumsky Canal was opened. This takes water from the Amu Darya, hundreds of kilometres before the river reaches the Aral Sea. The water is used to help desert people in Turkmenistan grow cotton.

This boat was one of the many left stranded in the desert when the Aral shoreline moved away from the port of Muynak.

Desert sea

The Karakumsky Canal and other **irrigation** projects have helped farmers in some areas, but they have made the land around the Aral Sea a desert. Fishing villages that were on the shoreline of the lake 30 years ago are now many kilometres from its shores. The land between the villages and the lake has dried up, leaving behind huge amounts of salt. Nothing will grow there. The lake and surrounding areas are very polluted. Many fishing boats are just rotting away.

FACTS

AREA	37 000 sq km
GREATEST LENGTH	350 km
GREATEST DEPTH	68 m
ALTITUDE	53 m
LOCATION	Kazakhstan, Uzbekistan

Changing nature

Just a few years ago the Aral Sea was teeming with fish. Now there is no fishing harvest and 24 species of Aral fish have died out. In the 1970s some people wanted to divert bigger Russian rivers to the area, to make up for the water already lost. But scientists realized that this would only make the situation worse. There are international discussions now to try to solve the Aral region's problems.

Lake Tanganyika

Tanganyika, in east Africa, is the seventh largest and second deepest lake in the world. It is the world's longest freshwater lake at 725 kilometres, yet its widest point is only 72 kilometres. The border between Zaire and Tanzania runs through the lake, while Burundi to the north and Zambia to the south have small parts of its shoreline.

Chimpanzee

B U R U N D I

Livingstone Memorial

Z A I R E

● **Kigoma**
● **Ujiji**

T A N Z A N I A

Hippopotamus

Lukuga

Elephant

Fish

Leopard

Crocodile

Flamingo

Snail

Black heron

Waterlilies

Z A M B I A

Local people live on the hillsides near the lake in Burundi. There has been a terrible war between the different peoples of this country in recent years.

Great Rift Valley

Lake Tanganyika lies at the lower end of East Africa's Great Rift Valley. The lake formed when this long, narrow trough filled with water millions of years ago. For most of the lake's length, the land rises steeply from its shores. The lake's only **outlet**, the River Lukuga, often becomes blocked by silt, which causes the lake's level to rise slightly.

Stanley and Livingstone

African tribes have lived near the lake's shores for thousands of years. The first Europeans to find Lake Tanganyika were Sir Richard Burton and John Hanning Speke, in 1858. They reached Ujiji, on the eastern shore, when searching for the source of the River Nile. In 1871, Henry Morton Stanley went in search of the Scottish explorer, David Livingstone, who had gone missing. After a difficult journey, Stanley found Livingstone at Ujiji and greeted him with the words, 'Doctor Livingstone, I presume?'

Kigoma, Tanzania's main port on the lake, is just 8 kilometres from the old fishing village of Ujiji. Today, timber, cotton and tobacco are shipped from Kigoma.

FACTS

AREA	32 900 sq km
GREATEST LENGTH	725 km
GREATEST DEPTH	1435 m
ALTITUDE	772 m
LOCATION	Burundi, Tanzania, Zaire, Zambia

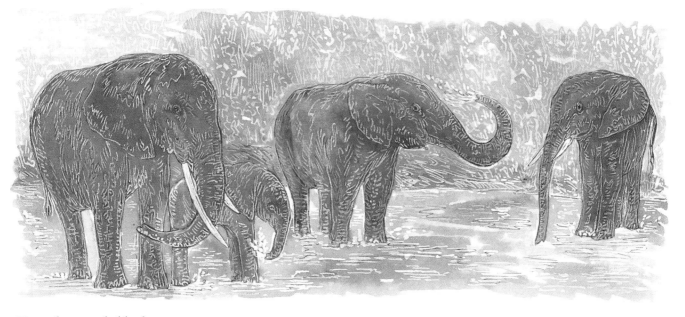

Rich wildlife

Many of Lake Tanganyika's fish are not found anywhere else in the world. This has happened because the lake is very old and has been separate from other bodies of water for a long time. Tanganyika is also home to hippopotamuses, crocodiles and large numbers of water birds. African elephants roam through the surrounding forests, and troops of chimpanzees live in the nearby **rain forest** of Zaire. The lake's beauty and wildlife are attracting tourists from all over the world.

Great Bear Lake

Great Bear Lake, in the Northwest Territories of Canada, is further north than the world's other large lakes. It lies right on the Arctic Circle, and is fed by melting snow. The lake drains into Great Bear River, a tributary of the Mackenzie River, which flows into the Arctic Ocean.

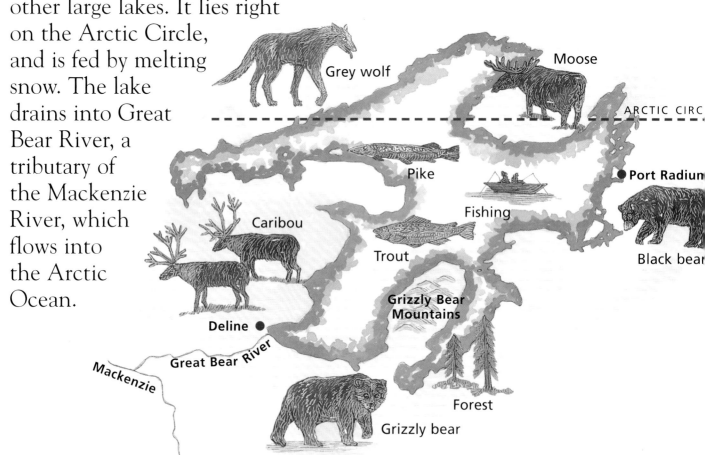

Grey wolf

Moose

ARCTIC CIRC

Pike

Fishing

Port Radiun

Caribou

Trout

Black bear

Grizzly Bear Mountains

Deline

Great Bear River

Mackenzie

Forest

Grizzly bear

In the far north

Great Bear Lake's climate is cold, and the lake is free of ice for only four months of the year. It is surrounded by the northern edge of Canada's taiga, a huge cold forest of evergreen trees. The first people to live here were Native American people called the Dene. In the Dene language, the lake is called Sahtu, meaning 'bear water'.

This crossing, at the edge of the lake near Deline, is open during the coldest months when the ice is thick. It links up with a normal road.

Fishing and mining

Great Bear Lake is famous for fishing. The world's largest lake trout was caught here in 1991. It weighed more than 30 kilograms. Great Bear Lake has many other fish, too, such as pike, grayling and whitefish. Visitors need a fishing **licence** to fish here and they return the catch to the lake after weighing it. On the eastern shore, pitchblende is mined at Port Radium. This mineral contains radium, which is used in hospitals, and uranium, which is used to make nuclear energy.

These huts are fishing lodges on an island in Great Bear Lake. They are open to fishing visitors and other holidaymakers during the summer months.

FACTS

AREA	31 800 sq km
GREATEST LENGTH	373 km
GREATEST DEPTH	411 m
ALTITUDE	119m
LOCATION	Canada

Arctic wildlife

The black bears and grizzlies which gave the lake its name, still roam around the area today. Black bears live in the forest and lowland areas, while grizzlies prefer the mountains. The region's other large animals are moose and caribou. Moose have always been very important to the Sahtu Dene people, providing them with meat and hides, as well as bones and antlers for tools. Bald eagles and golden eagles are also found in the region.

Lake Baikal

Lake Baikal lies in south-eastern Russia, just north of Mongolia. It is the deepest lake in the world, and holds more water than any other freshwater lake. More than a fifth of the world's fresh water is in this lake. With 336 rivers flowing into it, Baikal has just one outlet, the River Angara. This is a **tributary** of the Yenisei, the world's fifth longest river.

Sturgeon

Golomyanka

Baikal Mountains

Baikal seal

OLKHON

Saw mill

Angara

Irkutsk

Forest

Shrimp

Ulan Ude

Trans-Siberian Railway

Selenga

Baikalsk

Papermaking plant

Ships are stuck once the lake has frozen in January.
The ice can be more than 1.5 metres thick in places,
and sometimes it cracks with a loud bang.

People of Baikal

The Baikal region is the traditional homeland of the Buryat people, and their land, Buryatia, forms one of Russia's 22 republics. The Buryats were once nomads, moving their felt tents around the southern shores of the lake. Now they mostly live in wooden houses, especially in winter. Then the lake freezes over for five months, and people fish through holes in the ice.

Unique seals and fish

Lake Baikal is about 25 million years old, and is home to some amazing species of wildlife that are not found anywhere else on earth. The world's smallest and only freshwater seal, the Baikal seal, lives here. The lake also contains many fish, including huge sturgeon that grow longer than the small seals. An unusual species of deep-water fish called golomyanka, or Baikal cod, is also found here. Unlike most fish, the Baikal cod gives birth to live young rather than laying eggs. In addition, Lake Baikal contains one third of the world's freshwater shrimps.

Siberian industry

Baikal's water was once famous in Russia for being clear and pure. Visitors came to drink and bathe in the lake. In recent years, industry has developed around the lake and pollution is now an increasing problem.

The papermaking plants, timber works, shipbuilders and fish-processing factories here are a danger to the **environment**. Local people and others are working to protect Lake Baikal, the world's largest body of fresh water.

This factory, on the southern shores of the lake at Baikalsk, processes pulp for making paper. Protesters have tried to stop the factory polluting the lake with its waste.

FACTS

AREA	30 500 sq km
GREATEST LENGTH	620 km
GREATEST DEPTH	1620 m
ALTITUDE	455 m
LOCATION	Russia

Lake Malawi

Most of Lake Malawi, which is also sometimes called Nyasa, lies within the east African country of Malawi. Some of the lake's waters belong to neighbouring Mozambique, and the border of Tanzania runs along its north-eastern shoreline. The lake is fed by 14 rivers and has one outlet, the River Shire, which joins the bigger Zambesi River and flows to the Indian Ocean.

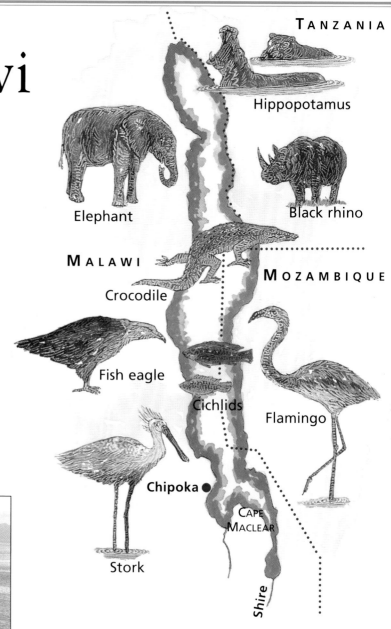

TANZANIA

Hippopotamus

Elephant

Black rhino

MALAWI

MOZAMBIQUE

Crocodile

Fish eagle

Cichlids

Flamingo

Chipoka

CAPE
MACLEAR

Stork

Shire

Ancient lake

Malawi is the third largest lake of the Great Rift Valley, after Victoria and Tanganyika. Fossils found in the region show that there was a lake here up to 120 million years ago. The present lake is more than 700 metres deep. Today, seasonal changes in rainfall cause the level of the lake to rise and fall slightly. During heavy rain, the lake fills up and prevents flooding. In the dry season, the lake goes on releasing water and stops rivers drying up.

This rocky inlet is at Cape Maclear, which juts into the southern end of Lake Malawi.

Fishermen's huts line this part of the lake's shore. Most Malawians are farmers, producing maize, rice, sugar cane and many other crops.

Lake of storms

When explorer David Livingstone reached the lake in 1859, he asked the local African people what it was called. They replied 'Nyasa', meaning 'lake', and so Livingstone named it Lake Nyasa. Later, the country that formed around its shores was called Nyasaland.

In 1964 the country's name changed to Malawi, which means 'broad water'. Livingstone also once called Lake Malawi the 'lake of storms'. From May to August, a south-easterly wind often blows up into a gale and creates high waves, making it look like the open sea.

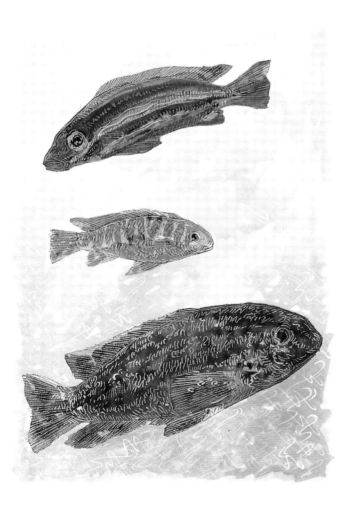

FACTS

AREA	29 600 sq km
GREATEST LENGTH	580 km
GREATEST DEPTH	701 m
ALTITUDE	472 m
LOCATION	Malawi, Mozambique, Tanzania

Fishing and sailing

Bantu tribes lived around the shores of Lake Malawi long before European explorers arrived. They lived on fish, which they caught in the lake using small boats. The lake has 200 different species of tropical cichlid fish. Today the fishing industry is based at the southern end of the lake. Passenger and cargo ships connect up with the railway at Chipoka. The ships carry cotton, rubber, rice and peanuts, as well as fish.

The world's lakes

The world's biggest lake, the Caspian Sea, lies between Europe and Asia. The other large lakes are spread across three continents – four in North America, three in Africa and two in Asia. But there are important lakes on the other continents too, and they are very different from each other.

Lake Eyre, Australia

Australia's largest lake does not usually have any water in it. The **desert** lands of South Australia are so hot and dry that Lake Eyre (right) is normally a huge area of mud covered with a crust of salt. This salt lake covers an area of 8900 square kilometres. In years which have very heavy rainfall, the lake fills with water. This has happened four times since 1950.

Lake Geneva, France and Switzerland

This is the largest of the lakes in the European Alps, and has an area of 577 square kilometres. Lake Geneva's northern shore is in Switzerland, and its southern shore is in France. The River Rhône enters the lake at one end and flows out at the other, on its way from the mountains to the Mediterranean Sea. The lakeside Swiss city of Geneva (left) was founded by the Romans. Its man-made fountain shoots a jet of water 145 metres above the surface of the lake.

Lake Titicaca, Peru and Bolivia

This large South American lake (right) lies in the Andes mountains on the border between Peru and Bolivia. At 3811 metres above sea level, it is the highest **navigable** lake in the world. Its shores and islands are home to the Aymara people, who live by farming and fishing in the lake using reed boats.

Loch Ness, Scotland

This long, narrow lake lies in a valley formed by a fault that runs right across Scotland. Loch Ness is 37 kilometres long and 3.2 kilometres across.

This lake is famous because people claim to have seen a monster in its deep waters. But all efforts to track down the monster have failed.

Glossary

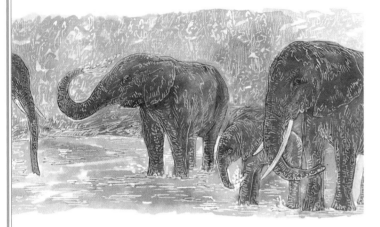

Elephants on the shore of an African lake.

altitude Height above sea level.

basin A hollow in the ground.

continent One of the Earth's huge land masses.

crust The Earth's outer shell.

dam A barrier built across a river, often used to make electricity.

delta The fan-shaped area at the mouth of some rivers, where the main flow splits into smaller channels.

desert A dry area of land where very little rain falls.

earthquake Movements in the Earth's crust that make the ground shake. Earthquakes can cause great damage.

environment The surroundings in which people, animals and plants live.

Equator An imaginary circle around the middle of the Earth.

fresh water Water that is not salty. Rain water and river water are fresh.

glacier A mass of ice that moves slowly like a river.

Great Rift Valley A long series of deep valleys in East Africa, caused by cracks in the Earth's surface.

gulf A stretch of water with a wide, curving shoreline.

harbour A sheltered place where ships load and unload.

irrigation Watering the land by means of canals and ditches.

lake bed The bottom of a lake.

Baikal seals playing in the water.

licence A certificate that allows you to do something, such as fishing.

lock Part of a canal or river that is closed off by gates so that the water level can be raised and lowered to let ships pass through.

mineral A solid substance that occurs naturally in the earth.

national boundary The border between different countries.

national park An area that people may visit where animals and plants are protected.

navigable Big and deep enough for large boats to sail on.

outlet A river into which the water from a lake flows.

plateau A flat area of high land.

pollution Damage caused by poisonous and harmful substances.

rain forest Thick forest found in warm tropical areas of heavy rainfall.

rapids Part of a river where the water moves very fast over rocks.

resource Something that people use to live or that can bring wealth when sold to others.

roe Fish eggs, used in caviar.

ruins Buildings from long ago that have fallen down and decayed.

salt-water Containing salt water, like the world's oceans and seas.

sea level The sea's surface, used as the level from which to measure heights above and depths below; some land and lakes are below sea level.

Tropical fish swimming in Lake Malawi.

settlement A place where people settle and live together.

skyscraper A very high building.

source The place where a river begins.

spring A flow of water that comes bubbling out of the ground to form a stream.

strait A narrow stretch of water between two areas of land.

trader A person who buys and sells goods.

transport Methods of carrying people and goods from one place to another.

tributary A small river that flows into a larger one.

tropical Found in the Tropics, the hottest part of the Earth near the Equator.

volcano An opening where molten rock and gas come from deep inside the Earth, often forming a mountain.

wigwam A home made of bark, reeds or skins spread over wooden poles. It looks like a round tent.

Sand dunes at Sleeping Bear National Park.

Index

Words in **bold** appear in the glossary on pages 30-31.